A *DISCOVER BOOK*

come to the island with me

TWO CHILDREN ENJOY GOD'S CREATION

By Mary Carpenter Reid

Illustrated by June Goldsborough

Copyright © 1992 Augsburg Fortress
Text copyright © 1992 Mary Carpenter Reid

All rights reserved. Except for brief quotations in critical articles or reviews, no part of this book may be reproduced in any manner without prior written permission from the publisher. Write to: Permissions, Augsburg Fortress, 426 S. Fifth St., Box 1209, Minneapolis, MN 55440

ISBN 0-8066-2632-1   LCCN 92-73012

Manufactured in the U.S.A.   AF 9-2632

96 95 94 93 92   1 2 3 4 5 6 7 8 9 10

Augsburg
MINNEAPOLIS

To sweet Clarice

One day a letter came from my cousin,
all about an invitation to go on a vacation.
I said *yes*! and got out my suitcase.

I put in . . .
    seven shirts, some shorts, sacks of special stuff,
    sunflower seeds for snacks,
    my snuggly sheep,
    a swimsuit, socks, and stacks of storybooks.
And then I put in two sticker books
—one for me and one for my cousin.
I put in my toothbrush, too.

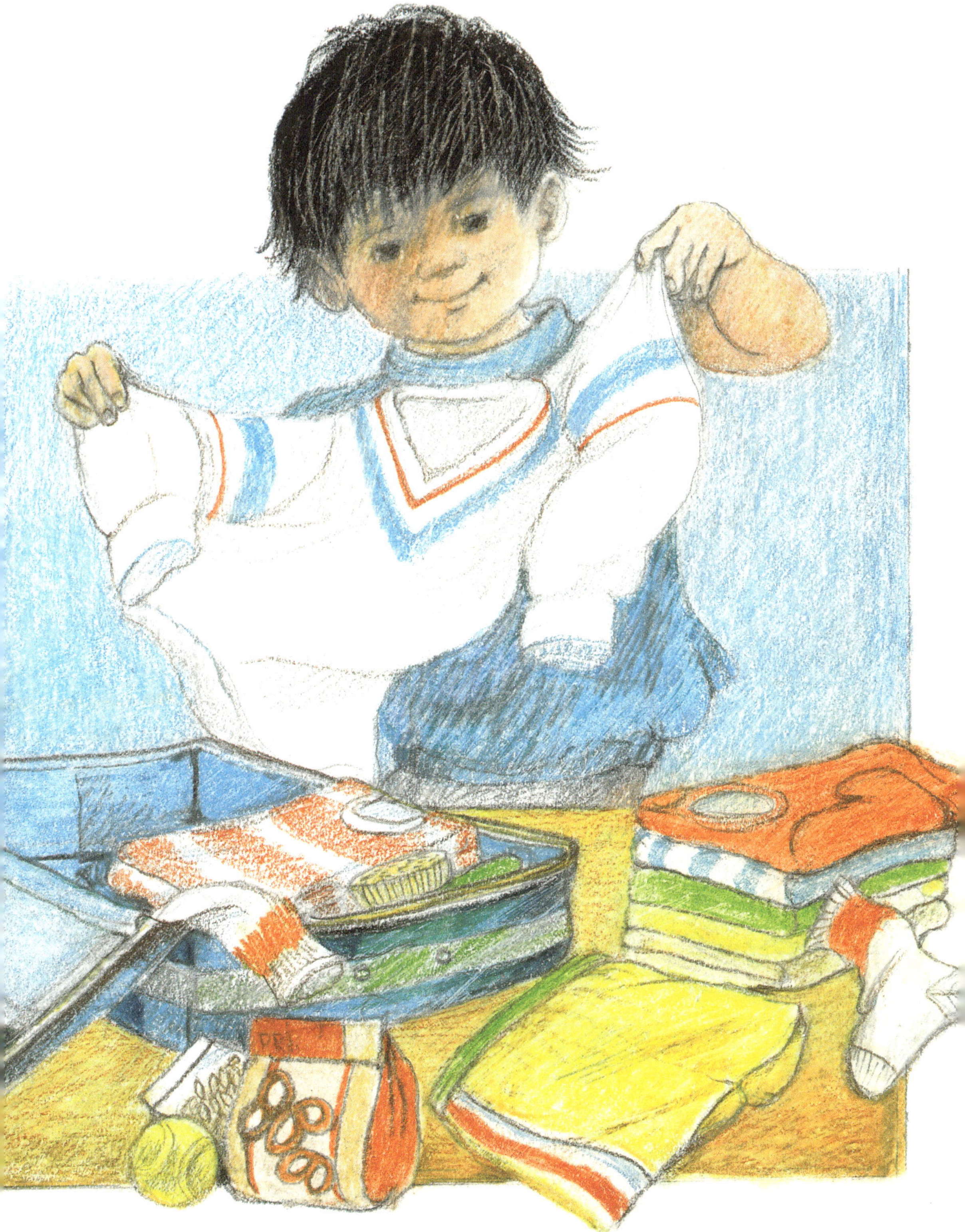

My cousin and I traveled to a wide, wide lake.
There were swings and slides for playing,
but we weren't staying,
because my cousin was taking me to an island
—an island out in the middle
of that wide, wide lake.

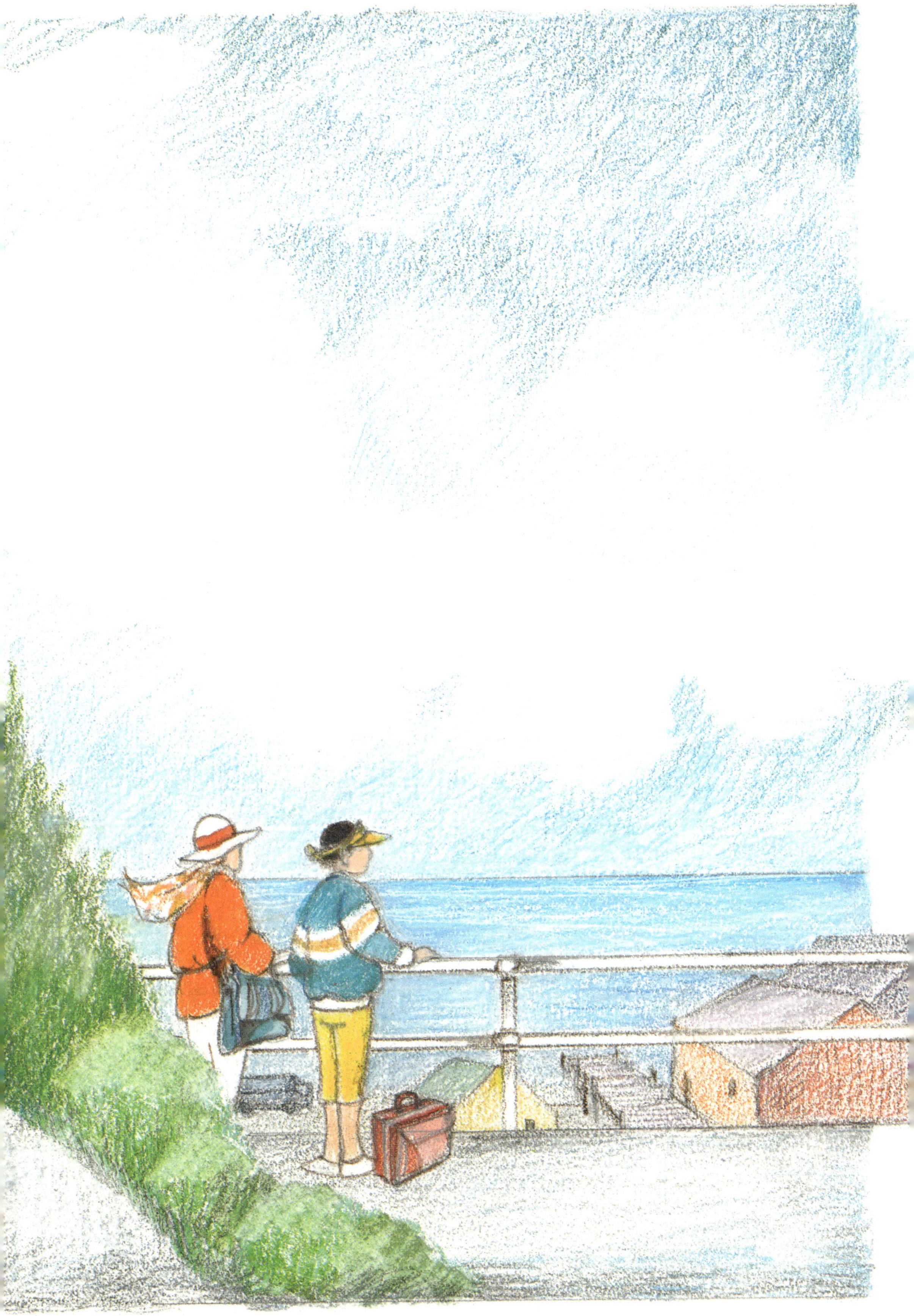

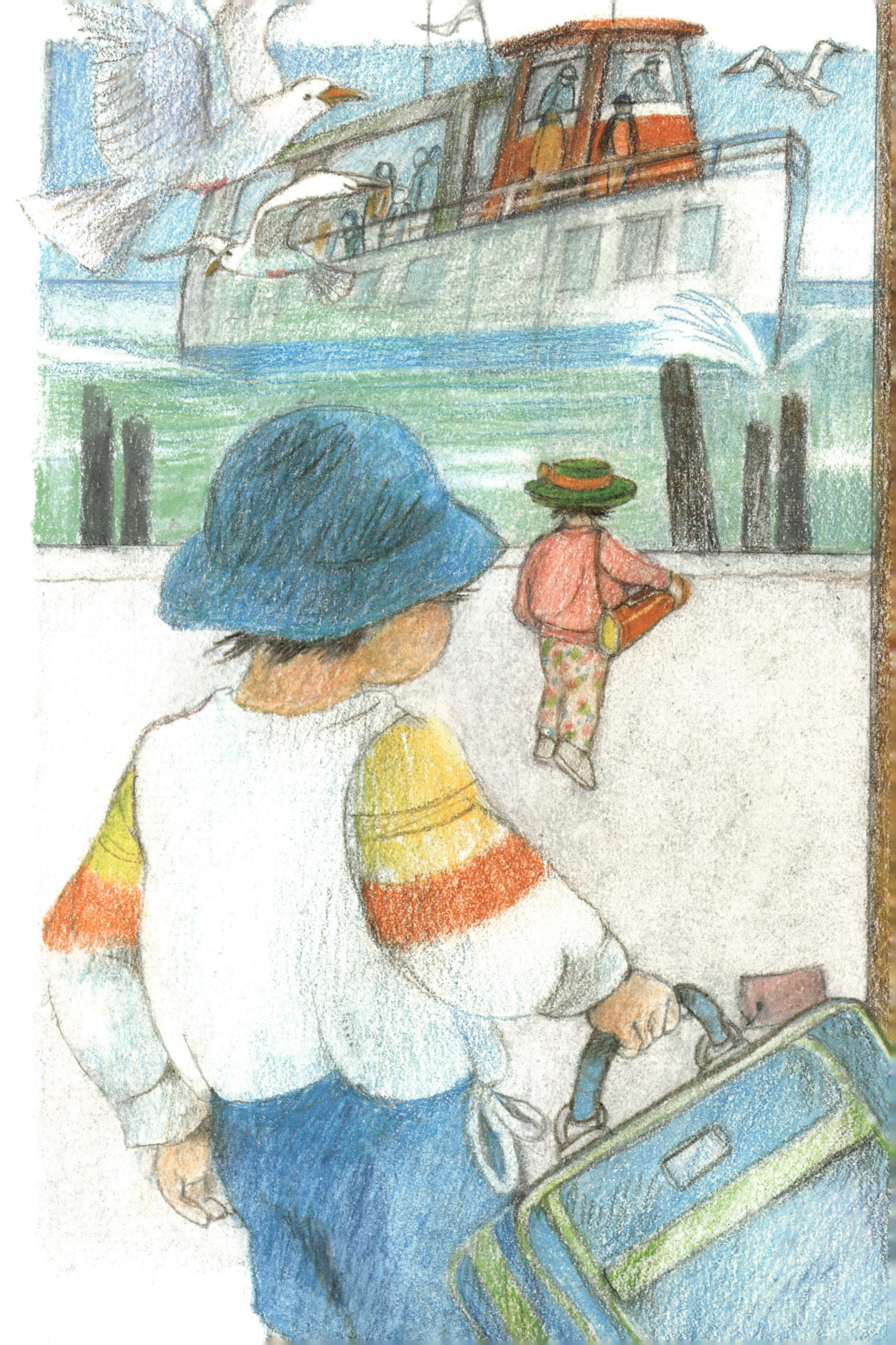

I looked, but I couldn't find a road to the island.
My cousin said, "Don't worry. I know how to get there."
I couldn't find a bridge to the island.
My cousin said, "Don't worry. I know how to get there."
I couldn't even find the island.
Then a big ferry boat blew its horn.

We hurried on board and climbed to the top deck.
The ferry boat turned and the water churned.
We stirred up foam that trailed away as we gathered speed and sailed away.

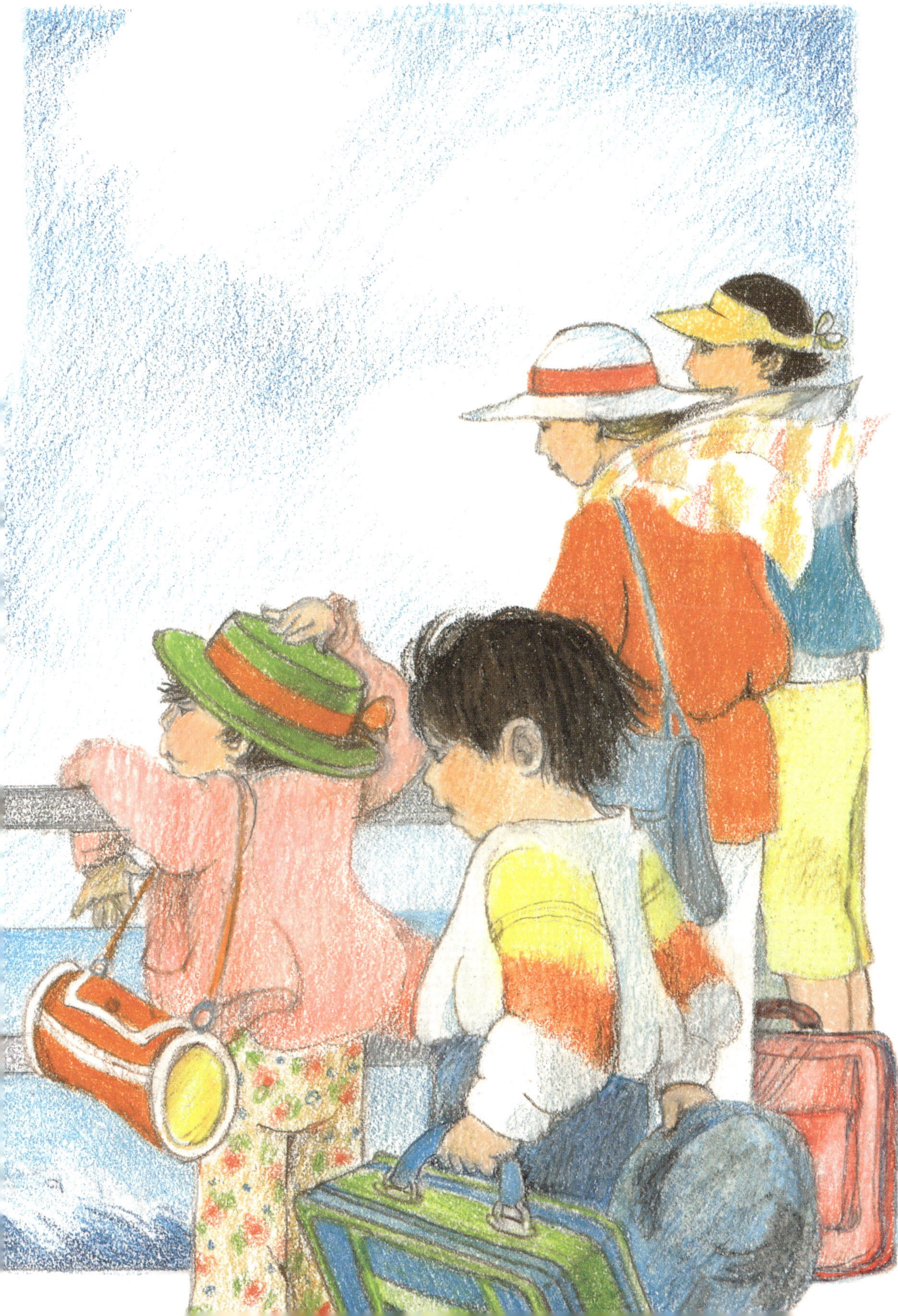

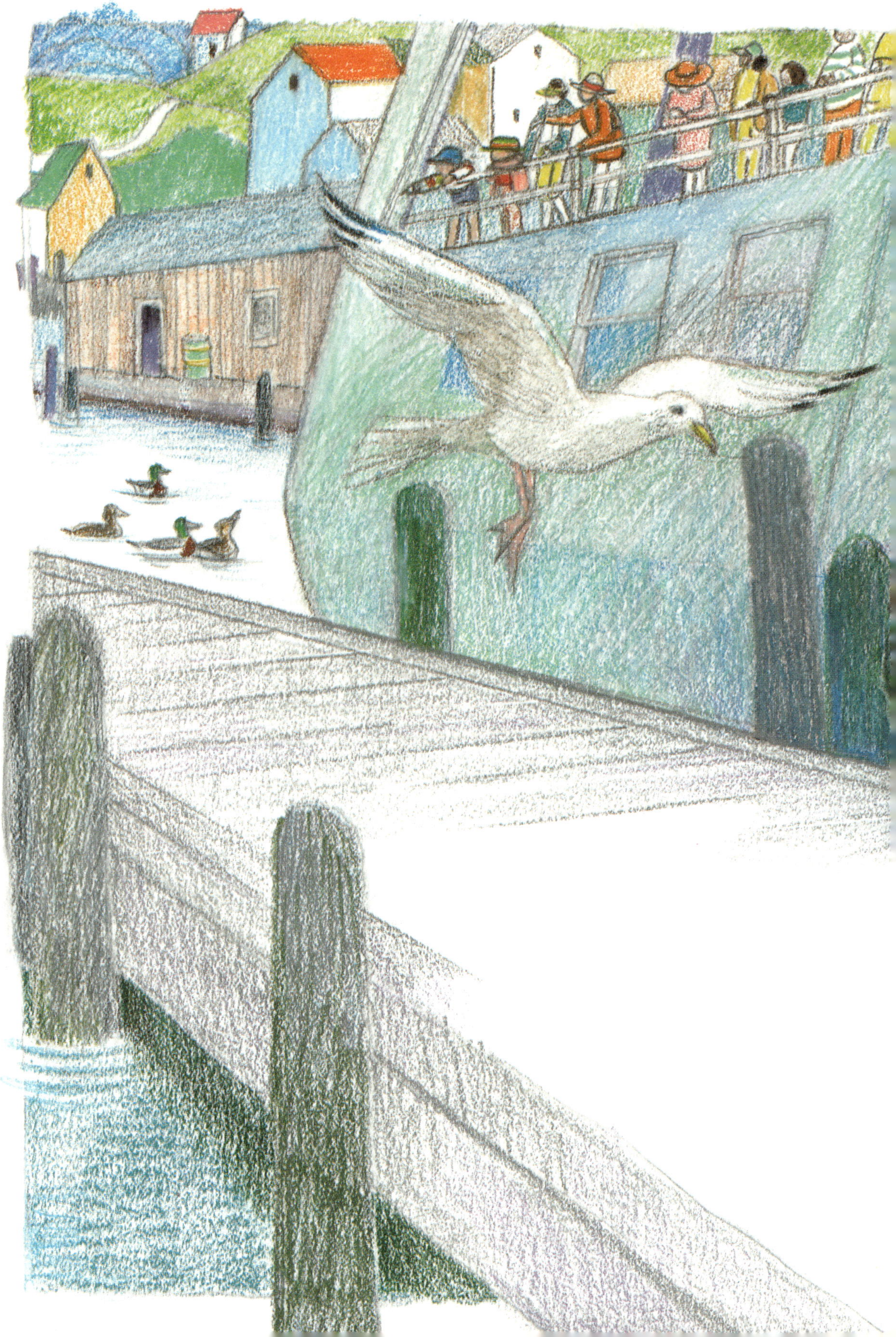

My cousin took me to *see* the island that God made.
The big ferry boat cuddled up to a dock
where a black cat climbed a post to meet us,
and four Mallard ducks swam over from their flock,
quack-quack-quacking as they came to greet us.

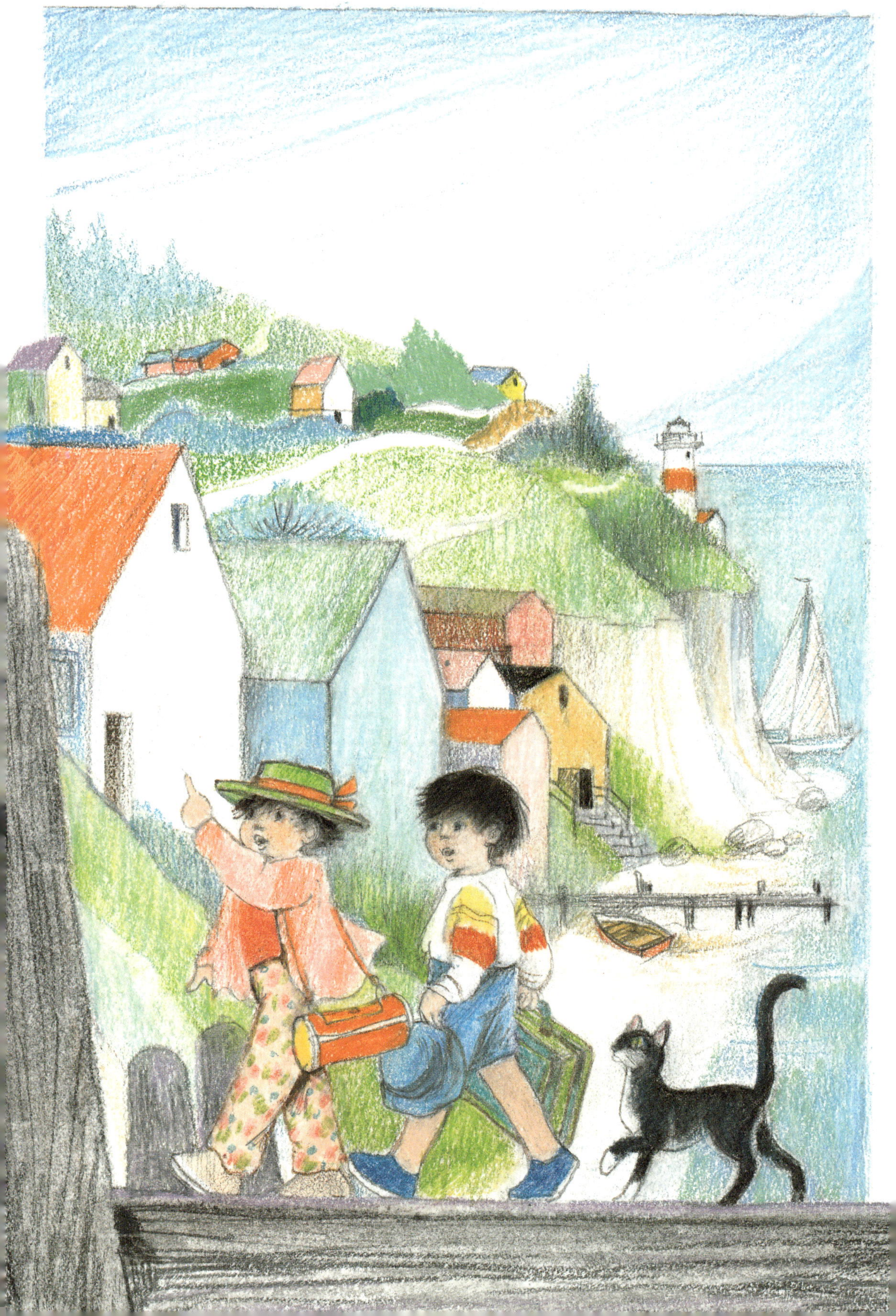

We *saw* trees and bushes and bright green grass,
small, almost-white rocks around the shore,
tall, almost-white cliffs above the shore—
shining as if rain had washed them clean,
and crisscross paths for us to explore.
And all around the island flowed a silver-blue circle
of water.

My cousin took me to *hear* the island that God made.
Doors banged in busy shops.
People talked, and gulls squawked.
Motorboats started with quick, soft pops.
There were no trains to rumble.
There were no buses to rattle,
no cars to roar.
But bicycles brushed by, and wings rushed by
as wild geese lifted and soared high
over the hotel where we would sleep.

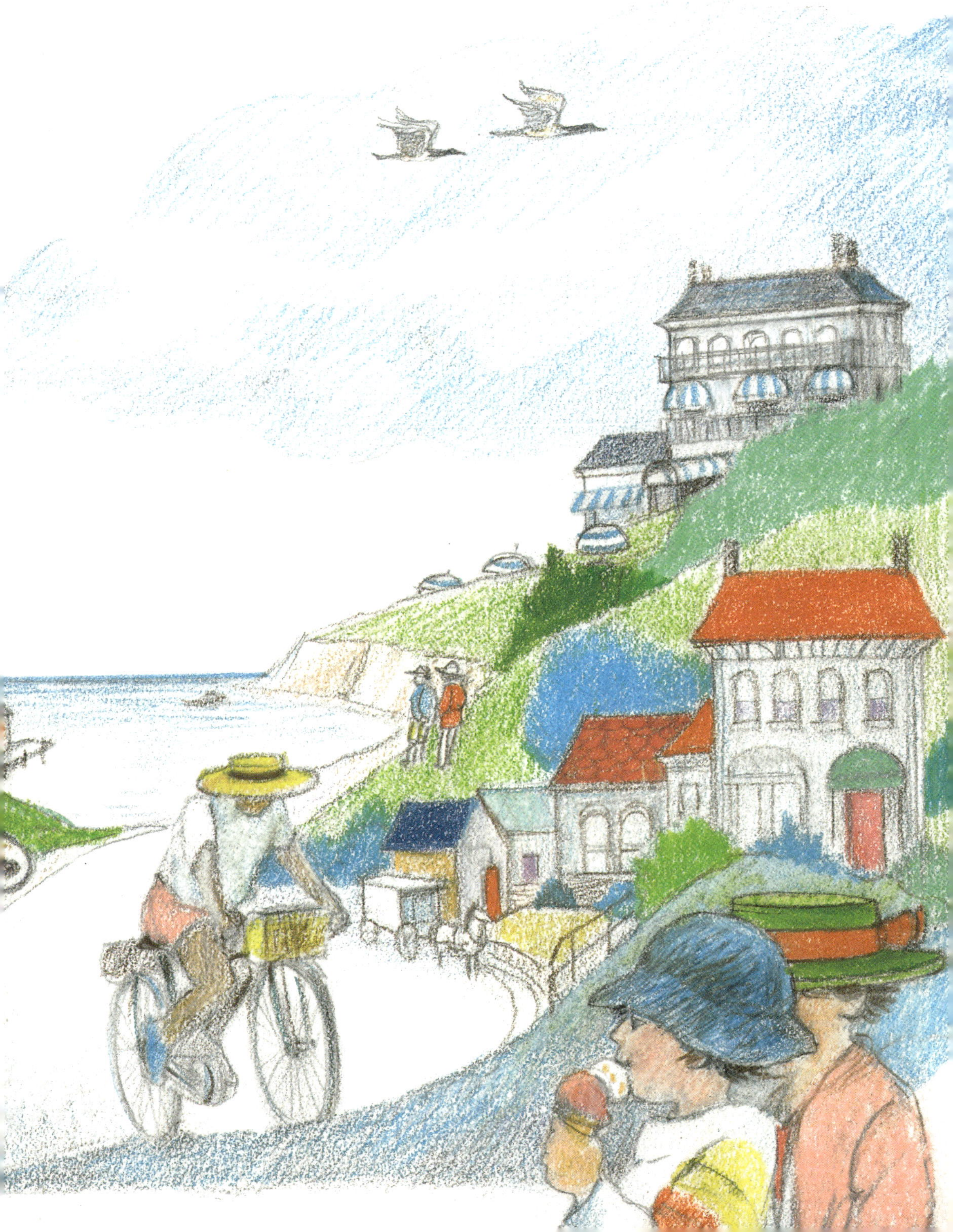

We *heard* fancy carriage wheels
and wide wagon wheels
and slim surrey wheels.
Horses pranced up the hill.
Their shoes *clop-clop, clop-clopped*.
We danced up the hill. Our shoes *clop-clop, clop-clopped*.

We tiptoed through the very grand lobby where grown-ups
gathered to take tea,
and held their cups just-so,
and chatted softly, so
not to miss a note of tea-time music.

And we cocked an ear, so
we could listen to the music
of birds that fluttered by the window.

My cousin took me to *smell* the island that God made.
We pretended to be secret agents sent to sniff
every smell on the island.
So we walked all the way around the island,
then over the top and back.
We walked all day.

We sniffed fir trees up in the woods,
sniffed strawberry plants out in the meadow,
sniffed a wild rose down by the water,
sniffed mint leaves over in the wet marsh.

We peeked inside a musty cave.
But what if something creepy lived there?
We ran.

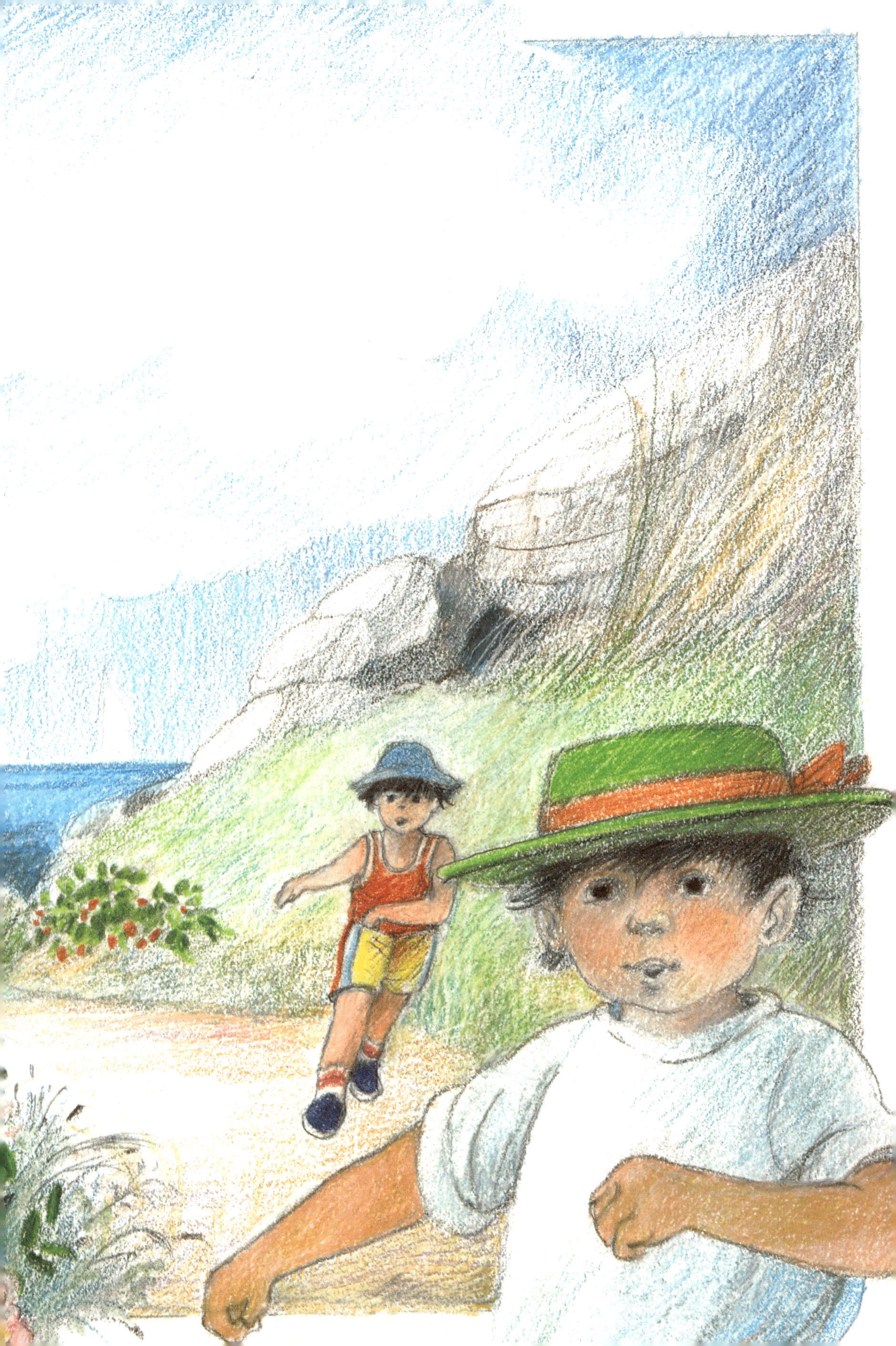

We hid low where cattails grow, and spied a Leopard Frog.
Suddenly we *smelled* honeysuckle in bloom,
but there was no honeysuckle there.
Then two women strolled near,
bringing so much honeysuckle perfume
that it trailed through the cattails like fog
and puffed over us and the Leopard Frog.
We just about choked.
The Leopard Frog croaked and leaped high in the air.
The women *shrieked*!
We giggled and crept out of there.

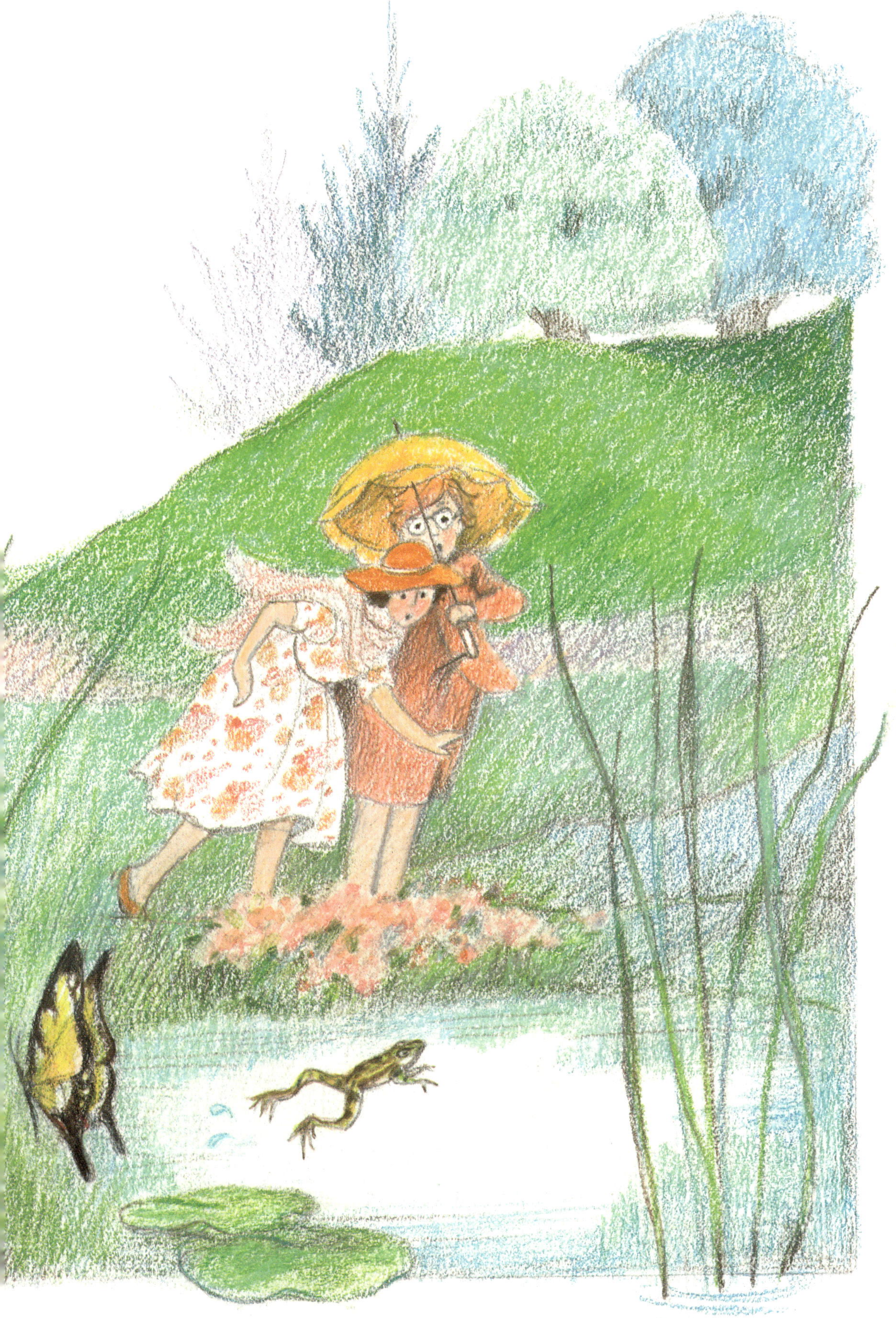

My cousin took me to *taste* the island that God made.
We climbed the highest hill, where a Red Squirrel
hunted pinecones to store away for a cold winter day.
The noon whistle *blew-ew-ew*.
Now, everyone on the island knew
it was time for lunch.

We ate soft cheese spread on bread,
crunched salty pretzels,
and bit into juicy blueberries that squirted blue.

A Yellow Warbler flew to a nest in a tree,
bringing lunch to baby birds that we couldn't see.
Maybe those birds knew about the noon whistle, too.

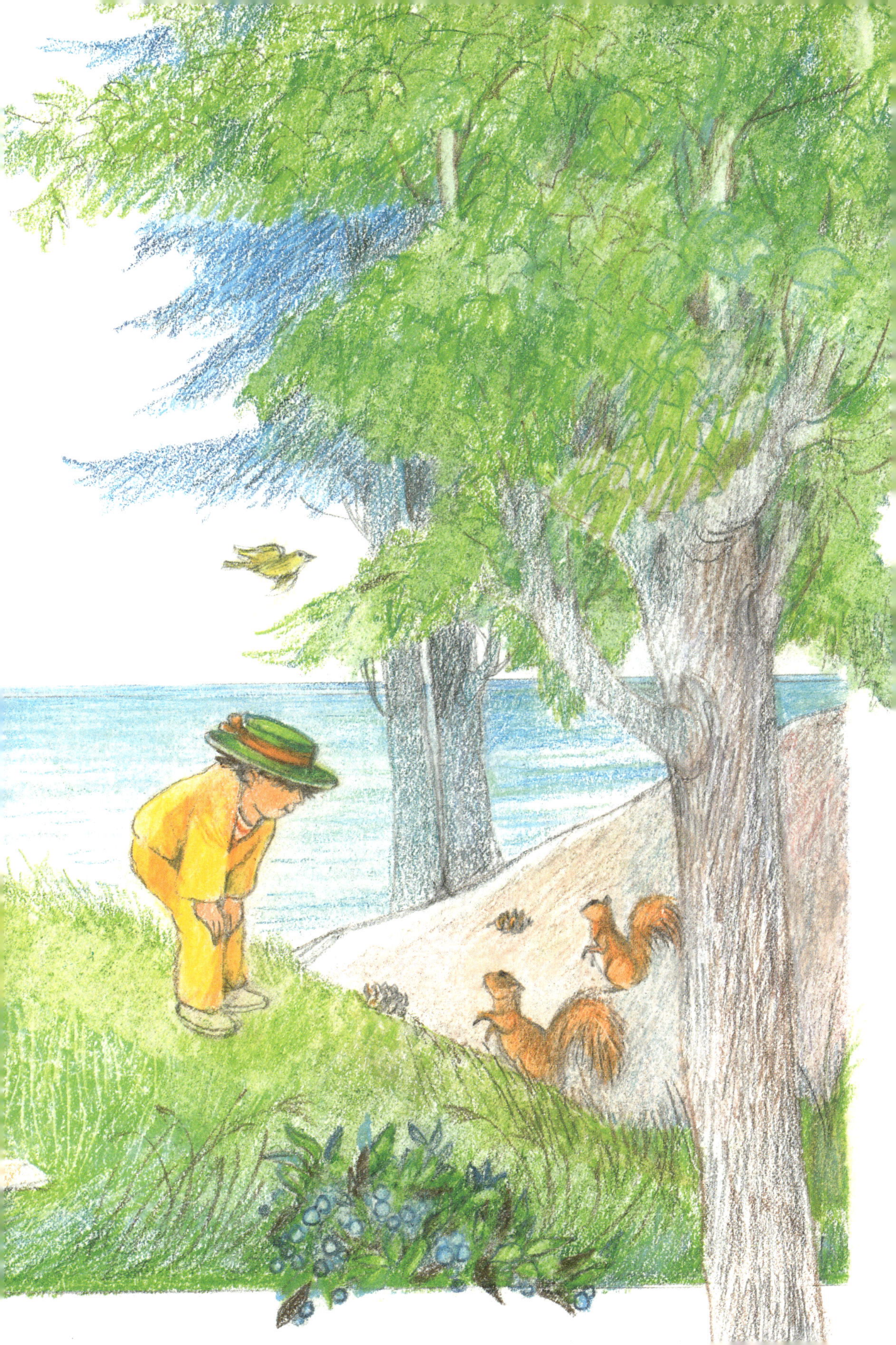

We slept in tall beds with ruffles above and ruffles below.
Before our prayers each night,
before we turned out the light,
we discovered tiny envelopes on our pillows.
In each tiny envelope was a thin chocolate mint.
We *tasted* them and wished for more.

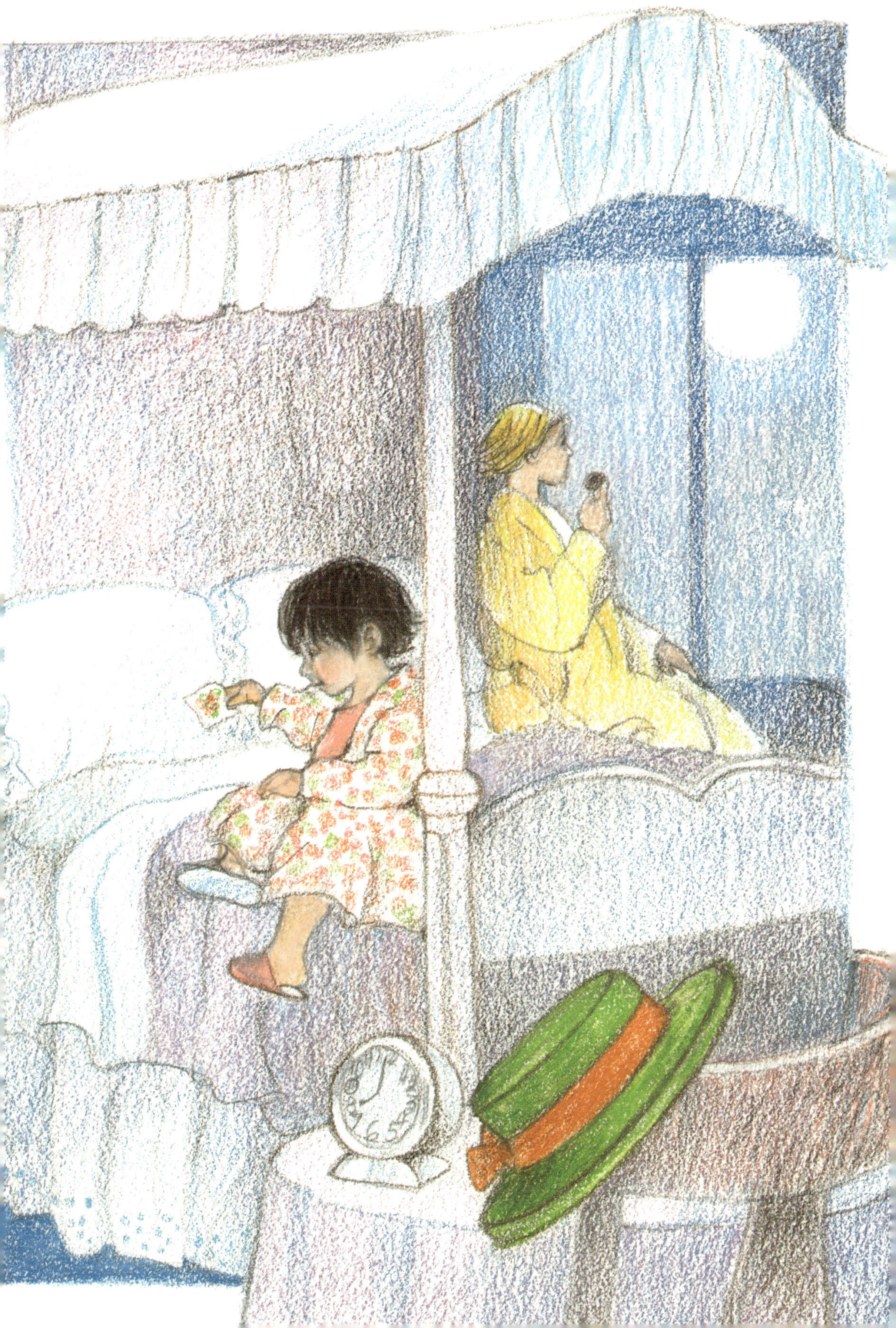

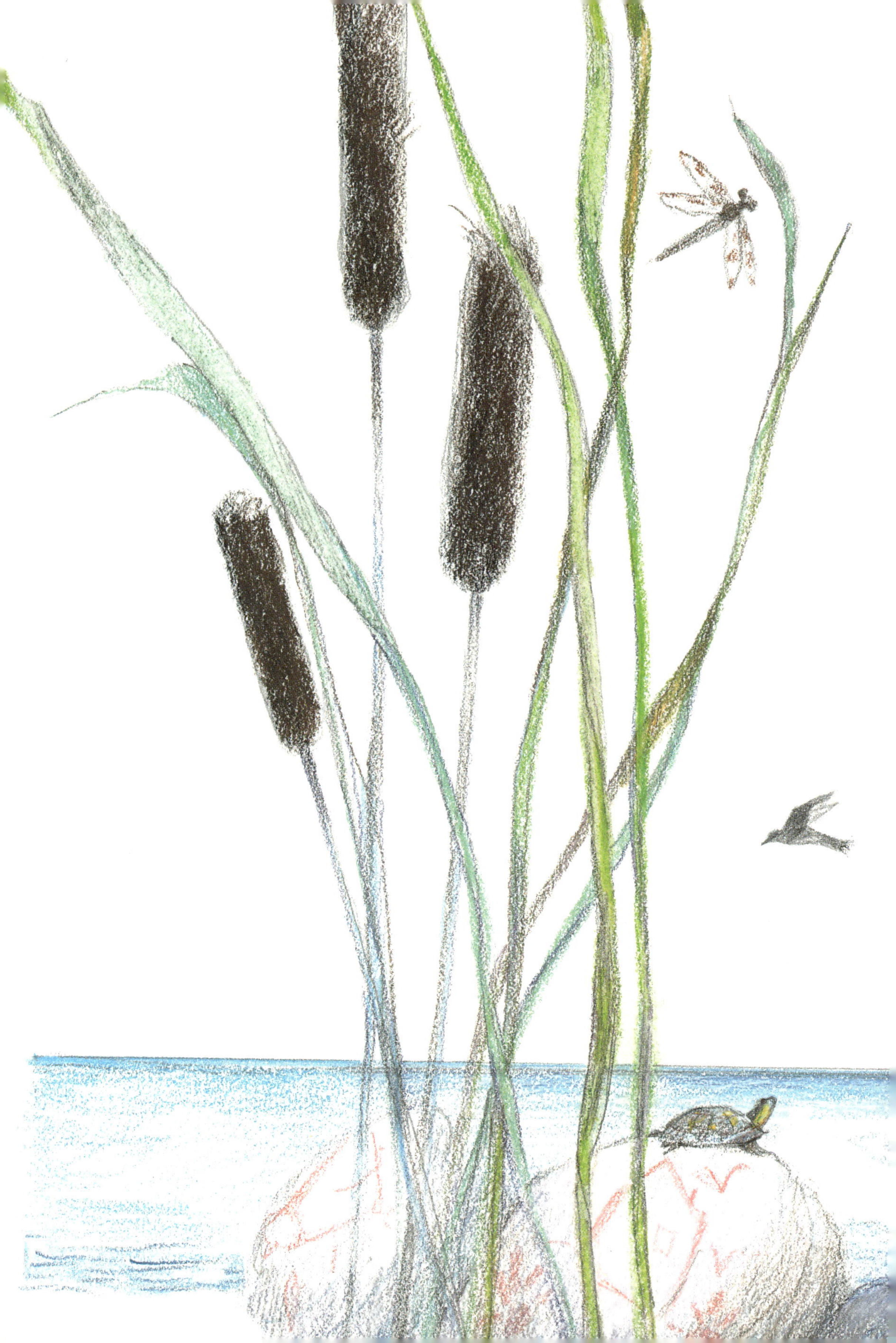

My cousin took me to *touch* the island that God made.
We didn't scratch our chigger bites, even though the
itches grew bigger.
We crushed red geranium petals and finger painted pale pink
pictures on almost-white rocks.
Down by the edge of the lake, we scooped up squishy mud.
We patted it and squeezed it
and built a magnificent mud island.
And the water flowed around it in a silver-blue circle.
We put a gull feather flag on top.

A wind rippled our gull feather flag,
a wind that *touched* our wet hands and feet
and spilled shivers over our arms,
and filled the air with crisp, little nips
that warned the Red Squirrel of snow soon to come,
and chilled the soft, silvery water
with a promise of hard, silvery ice.
It was time for us to leave the island.

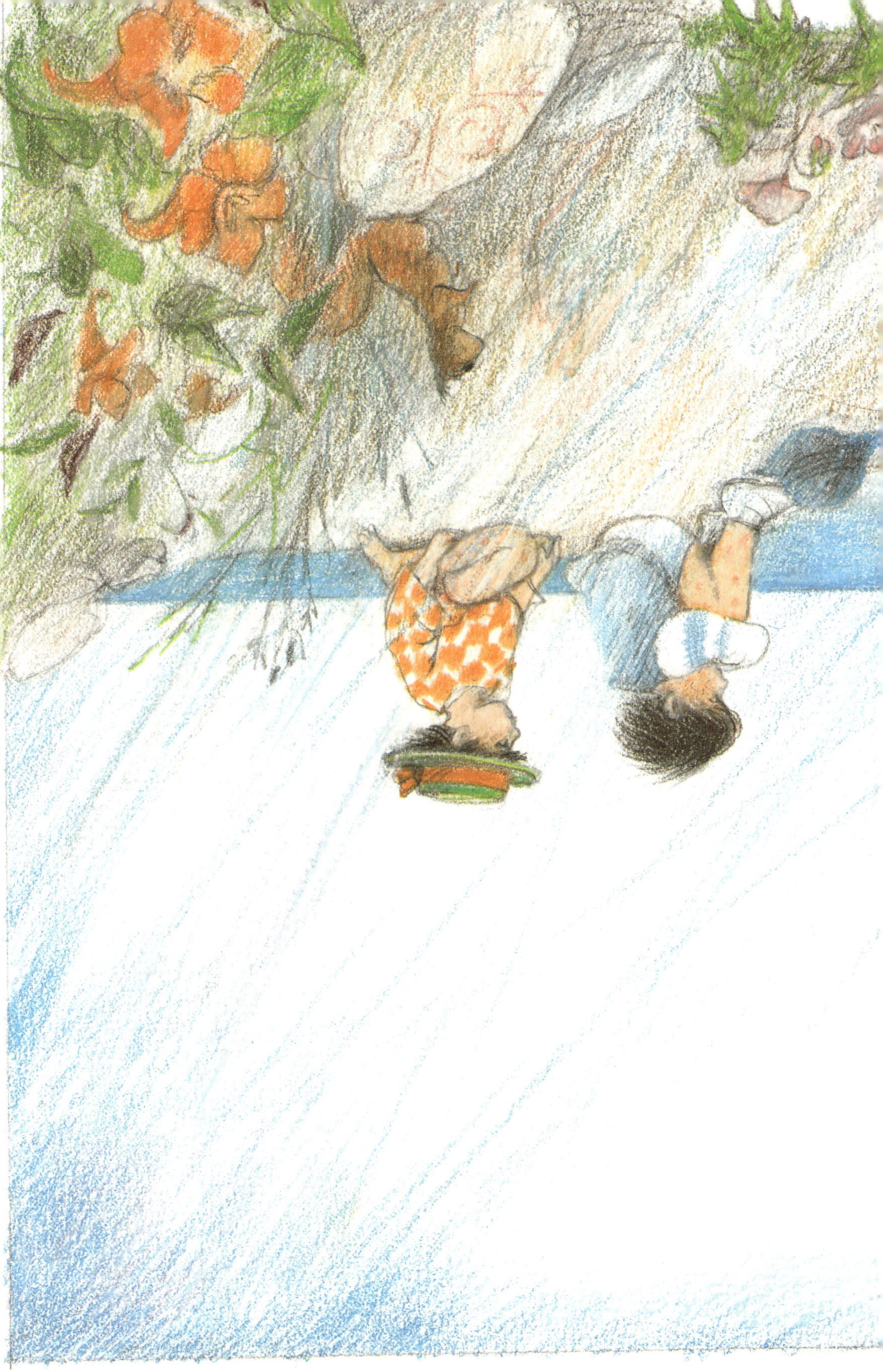

A chilly wind blew as we climbed on the big ferry boat.
My cousin and I . . .
    Had *seen* the island.
    Had *heard* the island.
    Had *smelled* the island.
    Had *tasted* the island.
    Had *touched* the island.
And we felt good in our hearts because we knew that
before the ice and snow come to the island,
God will dress the Red Squirrel in a warm winter coat.